QUEE.
ELIZABETH I

*One of the great achievements of Elizabeth I was that
she lived to die a natural death in an age when many of
her royal contemporaries met untimely ends. Despite
her sex she established and maintained her authority
and won the hearts and affections of her people.
Gloriana reigned in dazzling majesty over an exciting
new age of exploration, discovery, artistic brilliance,
architectural achievement and foreign conquest.*

Princess Elizabeth

*E*lizabeth's mother was Anne Boleyn; her father Henry VIII. On 7 September 1533, in the royal manor house at Greenwich, Queen Anne was brought to bed. The letter to the King announcing the birth of a prince had already been written and signed. How bitterly then must Elizabeth have disappointed both her parents.

Besides the fact of her gender, another important influence in shaping the character of the future queen was the loneliness and isolation in which she spent so many of her earlier years. Of course in that age royal children could expect to see little of their parents, but Elizabeth saw less than most. Christened in the church of the Franciscan Observants at Greenwich, with Cranmer for her godfather, she was, at the age of three months, given her own establishment at Hatfield which became from then until her accession to the throne her principal residence. But even as a princess she travelled about and lodged in other royal manors from time to time. In May 1536 her mother was beheaded. Henry had his marriage with Anne dissolved and Elizabeth, declared a bastard, excluded from the succession, and kept at a safe distance from his person.

In October 1537 Henry's third wife, Jane Seymour, gave birth to the long awaited prince. Edward and Elizabeth were both given the best available tutors, and were schooled in the same sort of learning. By the age of ten the little princess was already being coached in Italian, French and Latin. Later she took up Greek as well. Such an education was not at that time usual for a girl.

This early training was to do Elizabeth good service in later years. When she was queen, her councillors and courtiers, the men who surrounded her, had perforce to respect her intellect. However much they may have wished at times to do so, they could never dismiss as the fond imaginings of a foolish woman the opinions of a queen who could on the spur of the moment give the Polish ambassador a very sound drubbing in fluent and faultless Latin! Though a mere princess, and by no means destined to rule, she was given the intellectual training appropriate to the son of a king.

When Henry died in January 1547 Elizabeth was not yet fourteen years of age. Her political education, commenced in her father's reign, was continued in that of her brother in a way that Henry would hardly have intended or approved. Religion at this point began to divide the Tudors. The boy king Edward's mentors, and consequently his policies, were Protestant. Elizabeth accepted the government's lead, but her half-sister Mary, daughter of Henry's first wife, did not. And so Mary became the hope of the conservatives and Catholics, while it was to Eliz-

abeth that the Protestants began to look to continue her brother's policies should he die before he became a man, which seemed ever more likely.

Elizabeth also at this time, as she grew to womanhood, began inevitably to attract the attentions of men for whom religion was secondary and the possession of power the major goal. One such man was Thomas Seymour, the ambitious younger brother of the Lord Protector Somerset, and uncle to the little King. Seymour's conspiracy to build up a strong political faction reached dangerous heights before it was toppled by the arrest and imprisonment of the key figures in it.

This was the dangerous moment for Elizabeth. Was she knowingly involved in Seymour's plot? She was rigorously interrogated, but kept her head, and, in her haughty reminders to her interrogators that she was indeed the King's sister and ought to be treated with due honour and respect, she showed some measure of that fighting spirit which was to stand her in good stead in many a later crisis.

Seymour went to the block. Elizabeth escaped, but learned the value of discretion. Never again did she let herself become so deeply involved in the ambitions of others.

LEFT:
Philip II of Spain married Mary Tudor but she died childless in 1558. He supported the succession of Elizabeth as queen but the two monarchs slowly and reluctantly became enemies when the balance of power in Europe seemed in danger of shifting.

BELOW:
Part of Visscher's panorama of London much as it was in Elizabeth's day, showing Old St Paul's after the spire was burned down.

*T*he death of Edward on 6 July 1553 threw England into turmoil, and for a time it looked as if Henry VIII's worst fears were about to be fulfilled.

And yet the people of England had on the whole scant sympathy with the schemes of would be usurpers anxious to take advantage of the death of the last male Tudor heir and displace both the daughters of Henry VIII. Looking back now with grateful recollection to the splendid days of Henry VIII 'of famous memory', they were determined that his daughters, whatever doubts there might be about their legitimacy or whatever misgivings about their religion, should inherit his throne. Mary threw herself unhesitatingly upon the affections of her people and they responded to her enthusiastically.

But, as Mary's policies unfolded and her people's initial enthusiasm evaporated, Elizabeth became inevitably the repository of all the hopes of all the discontented. Those who shrank from a persecuting catholicism as revealed in the fires of Smithfield, and those who resented the ever-increasing subjection of English to Spanish interests which followed Mary's marriage to Philip II, King of Spain, began to take comfort from the knowledge that Mary was childless and that Elizabeth would in time succeed. Elizabeth, they fully expected, would be a Protestant and a national queen, and, whether she liked it or not, this was the character into which she

Here is my hand,
My dear lover England,
I am thine both with mind
and heart,
For ever to endure,
Thou mayest be sure,
Until death us two do part.
WILLIAM BIRCH, 1559

could raise for a maiden queen. It was, of course, expected in that male-dominated age that such a queen would take a husband. It was unthinkable that a mere woman should endeavour, unsupported by a consort, to manage the business of a kingdom on her own. And when she married it was also naturally supposed that the queen would be guided and directed in large measure by the will and policies of her husband. And if, as in the case of Mary, that husband was an alien sovereign with dominions of his own to attend to, it was almost inevitable that the interests of his wife's realm should be subordinated to those of his own. So it was with Philip and Mary, as Elizabeth saw and noted. Her own independent spirit would not take kindly to the thought of being ruled by any man, and she could see that England took equally unkindly to the influence of an alien monarch. When her own turn came and her subjects pressed her to marry, she would remember how Mary had fared.

The second lesson which Mary's reign taught Elizabeth was how inevitably and dangerously the forces of discontent within the kingdom would gather round the person of the accepted heir.

found herself forced by the pressure of events.

To look forward for relief to Elizabeth's accession was no crime. The danger for Elizabeth came rather from those who were not content to wait for that relief but wished to hasten its arrival. One such was Thomas Wyatt who in January 1554 rose in rebellion against Mary's proposed match with Philip.

Letters from Wyatt to Elizabeth were discovered and the princess found herself under grave suspicion. She was sent to the Tower and was in real danger of her life for her entry into that fortress was made, rather ominously, through the Traitors' Gate. But discretion proved its worth. If Elizabeth had ever given Wyatt an answer it had only been by word of mouth, and no proof of any criminal complicity could be found. After two months of interrogation and imprisonment in the Tower, she was transferred to a less rigorous detention at the royal manor of Woodstock.

From the events of Mary's reign Elizabeth learned two valuable lessons, ones that she herself was to refer back to more than once in later years. In the first place she came to appreciate something of the magnitude of the problems that the question of marriage

*E*lizabeth was at Hatfield in November 1558 when the news of Mary's death was brought to her. Six days later she moved to London which she entered in procession amid general rejoicings. It was confidently anticipated that the new reign would see the end of the burning of heretics and relieve England of the Spanish incubus. The optimistic atmosphere which normally surrounds the accession of a new sovereign, raising hope that old wrongs will be righted and fresh starts made, was enhanced in Elizabeth's case by the general expectation that this still young princess (she was only 25) would raise to power a new generation of men, closer in age and outlook to her than the old guard of councillors who had dominated the political scene in the previous reign.

Surprising as it later seemed, it was Philip of Spain who was chiefly responsible for persuading his dying wife to endorse the succession of the half-sister she hated. The King of Spain had indeed no alternative but to support the claims of Elizabeth, for the English succession had by now become a European political question of major proportions.

If Elizabeth were, as the Papacy said she was, illegitimate, and had therefore no title to the English throne, then the heir to Mary of England was in all probability that other Mary, Mary of Scotland, granddaughter of Henry VIII's eldest sister Margaret. But in

RIGHT:
Mary Queen of Scots, by a follower of Clouet.

BELOW:
Part of a tapestry supposed to have been worked by Mary in Hardwick Hall during her years of captivity.

April 1558 the young Queen of Scotland had been married to the heir to the throne of France, and it was confidently expected that this marriage would lead in time to the union of the two kingdoms. If to this dual heritage Mary Stuart were now to add the throne of England as well, the balance of power in Europe would be seriously disturbed, and Philip would find a barrier of potentially hostile territories erected across his vital sea communications between the two most important of his many dominions, the Netherlands and Spain. Rather than let this happen it was better that Elizabeth, illegitimate and poten-

tially heretical though she might be, should succeed to the English throne. She was, after all, as yet unwed, and could perhaps be found a husband, even Philip himself, who would keep her and her kingdom within the Spanish sphere of influence.

And so when, on 17 November 1558, Mary died, Elizabeth was immediately proclaimed Queen and a new era of religious tolerance began. In the short term the religious question was settled by the passage of the Acts of Supremacy and Uniformity in her first parliament, and in the long term by Elizabeth's steadfast refusal to consider any further changes.

Later there was the dark shadow of the penal laws and the savage treatment meted out to so many of the priests of the Catholic mission who were at work for the reconversion of England from 1574 onwards. There was also the sad tragedy of Mary of Scotland who fled to England for refuge from her own rebellious subjects in 1568, spent more than eighteen years a prisoner and in the end was executed to satisfy the clamour of Elizabeth's loyal and anxious subjects. But Mary was repeatedly involved in plots to kill or depose Elizabeth, and only the Queen's reluctance to see a crowned head fall had saved her from a much earlier death. And however unbiassed the Catholic mission was originally intended to be it could not but appear to Elizabeth's councillors as just another part of a sustained political campaign of the Papacy against the English Queen, and be associated in their minds with the Bull of deposition of 1570, the armed invasions of Ireland in 1579 and 1580, and the papal support for the Spanish Armada of 1588. It was as destroyers of the loyalty of the Queen's subjects that the Catholic priests were made to suffer.

Fridericus Hulsius inventor et sculpsit.

Somerviles haste to Kill the Queene.

Queen Elizabeth Dancing with Robert Dudley, Earl of Leicester, *by an unknown artist, shows how the Queen liked to 'dance high, in the Italian style', especially when partnered by her favourite.*

The most urgent problem of the new reign was that of the succession. This was a far-reaching question which, of course, included the more specific but equally important question of whom Elizabeth would marry. If she married and had a child then all uncertainty about the future would be dispelled. But should she die before that happy event (and as early as 1562 the smallpox nearly carried her off), then there would be a very real and dangerous uncertainty about who should be her successor. And so her faithful parliaments time and again urged upon the Queen, and at no time more insistently than in the sessions of 1563 and 1566, the need to marry, or at least to nominate her heir.

Whether Elizabeth ever seriously considered taking a husband is one of the great enigmas of her career. Suitors for her hand ranged in rank from the King of Spain himself down to her early favourite Sir Robert Dudley, and included at one time or another two sons of the Holy Roman Emperor, two brothers of the King of France, the Crown Prince of Sweden, and the Earls of Arran and Arundel, but only a few stood much of a chance. The French princes, for example, were never really seriously in the running, and yet with Francis, the younger of the two, who was successively Duke of Alençon and Anjou, she managed to play out the game for more than a decade and played it so skilfully that she had some of her English councillors very worried indeed.

More seriously entertained was the earlier candidature of the Archduke Charles, one of the sons of the Emperor Ferdinand I, and a first cousin of Philip of Spain. From 1559 to 1567 his virtues were urged upon the Queen from time to time, most urgently by those

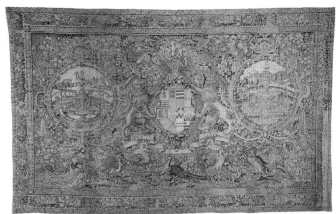

already resolved to avoid their fates by living and dying unwed.

Probably the only real love of Elizabeth's life was her affection for Robert Dudley which in the years 1559–61 flamed into a passion so powerful that her heart very nearly overruled her head. The difficulty with Dudley was twofold; he had a wife, and he had jealous political rivals who would bitterly resent his promotion to the position of consort. The wife (Amy Robsart) was eliminated in 1560 when it was said that she had fallen downstairs and broken her neck, but there were rumours of foul play. Elizabeth could not have married the widower without tongues wagging and her regal radiance being badly tarnished.

The moment passed, and reason prevailed. Elizabeth raised Dudley to the peerage as Earl of Leicester and continued to repose confidence in his counsel, but showed her political detachment by offering him to the widowed Mary of Scotland as a suitable second husband.

ABOVE:
One of a set of tapestries commissioned by the Earl of Leicester for the Queen's apartments at Kenilworth.

BELOW:
An engraving of one of the Queen's visits to Kenilworth Castle, the seat of her favourite, the Earl of Leicester.

who were jealous of the ascendancy of Dudley and feared he would win the Queen for himself. But there were two obstacles in the way of the Archduke's success which were in the end to prove insuperable. In the first place Elizabeth refused to commit herself until she had actually seen him and satisfied herself that the rumours which had reached her about his physical deformity were not true. The Archduke, for his part, as adamantly refused to come to England until he was assured of acceptance. To present himself for inspection and then to be turned down was a personal humiliation he was not prepared to risk. By 1567 when Elizabeth at last broke off the negotiations she had seen the tragic consequences of Mary of Scotland's marriage to Lord Darnley. She would remember also the unhappy consequences of her sister's marriage to Spanish Philip. Perhaps she had

Queen Elizabeth going in Procession to Blackfriars in 1600, *by Robert Peake. The Queen is preceded by six Knights of the Garter, from left to right Lord Sheffield, Lord Howard of Effingham, the Earl of Cumberland, Lord Hunsdon, an unknown, and the Earl of Shrewsbury. The background suggests several properties connected with the Earl of Worcester, Elizabeth's then Master of the Horse, who may well have commissioned the painting.*

The tilting armour of Sir Henry Lee, who was the originator of the Accession Day Tilts probably in 1572.

Elizabeth's public image remained untarnished, and this was the great secret of her success. She was expert at presenting herself to her people in the best light. She made repeated public progresses through her kingdom and displayed an ostentatious interest in the welfare of even the meanest of her subjects as she passed. Impromptu speeches to the thronging spectators, the good humoured receiving of even the coarsest but well-intentioned gesture of goodwill, the spectacle of majesty riding in state in a litter borne by great noblemen – these, and many similar touches, contributed to the building up of the legend of Elizabeth.

On one visit to Lord North of Kertlinge in 1578, which lasted 3 nights and 2½ days, the following expenditure was incurred by the host:

74	hogsheads of beer	£32. 7s. 6d.
6	hogsheads of claret	£27
20	gallons of sack	£2. 13s. 4d.
32	swans	£10. 13s. 4d.
34	pigs	£1. 14s.
32	geese	£1. 12s.
4	stags and 16 bucks, gulls, snipe, plovers, curlews, oysters, 8 dozen crayfish, herring.	

Entertainments, gifts and gratuities.

Total expenditure	£762. 4s. 2d.

The cult of Gloriana was the result of a deliberate and skilful move to replace the pre-Reformation festivals and ceremonies of Corpus Christi, Easter and Ascensiontide, based on the Virgin Mary and saints.

The new festivals of the Virgin Queen's Accession Day and birthday took their place and ensured that the people did not suffer from any decrease in ritual and public display to which they could look forward.

Accession Day festivities, which took place each 17 November, were both courtly and popular. Prayers, sermons, bell-ringing, bonfires and feasting – all were used as expressions of joy by Elizabeth's subjects that she was their monarch.

The Queen combined business with pleasure during her summer holidays. She would go on an easy perambulation of the country, lasting for one or two months, during which she would accept hospitality from the gentry or from towns. The Spanish ambassador described the scene on a progress in 1568: 'She was received everywhere with great acclamations and signs of joy, as is customary in this country; whereat she was extremely pleased and told me so, giving me to understand how beloved she was by her subjects and how highly she esteemed this, together with the fact that they were peaceful and contented, whilst her neighbours on all sides are

ABOVE:
George Clifford, 3rd Earl of Cumberland, as Queen's Champion at the Tilt, in a miniature by Hilliard, c.1590.

BELOW:
A tilt yard, showing the judges seated in a box from which they could keep the score of lances shattered. Stands for outsiders to see the solemnities on payment of one shilling were also provided.

ABOVE:

Procession of Knights of the Garter, *1576, engraved by Marcus Gheeraerts the Elder. Such processions took place on St George's Day. This one is led by the Verger of the Chapel of St George at Windsor, followed by thirteen Poor Knights of Windsor, pursuivants, heralds, Knights both English and foreign, officers of the Order and Elizabeth preceded by two gentlemen ushers and a nobleman bearing the sword. By 1595 the Garter festival had assumed such popularity that the procession made its way three times around the courtyard, so that all might see the Queen.*

in such trouble. She attributed it all to God's miraculous goodness. She ordered her carriage sometimes to be taken where the crowd seemed thickest, and stood up and thanked the people.'

Great preparations were made for a visit from the Queen, ranging from rubbish clearance and street cleaning to the memorizing of speeches and preparation of pageants. In addition a silver-gilt cup would be purchased for presentation to the Queen, and money placed inside it according to the wealth of the town. J. E. Neale records that Coventry put a hundred pounds in its cup, and Elizabeth 'was pleased to say to her Lords, "It was a good gift, £100 in gold; I have but few such gifts." To which the Mayor answered boldly, "If it please your Grace, there is a great deal more in it." "What is that?" said she. "It is," said he, "the hearts of all your loving subjects." "We thank you, Mr Mayor," said she; "it is a great deal more indeed." '

To the end of her long reign Queen Elizabeth kept the custom of going on progresses as it enabled her to see as many of her people as could possibly flock from the countryside and line the roads through which she passed. Her 'Golden Speech' to the Commons on 30 November 1601, her last as it turned out, is ample evidence of the affection she felt for her people and the humility with which she served them.

'Though God hath raised me high, yet this I count the glory of my crown, that I have reigned with your loves. This makes me that I do not so much rejoice that God has made me to be a queen, as to be a queen over so thankful a people.... Neither do I desire to live longer days, than that I may see your prosperity, and that is my only desire.... Of myself I must say this, I never was any greedy, scraping grasper, nor a strait fast-holding prince, nor yet a waster; my heart was never set on worldly goods, but only for my subjects' good.... Yea mine own properties I count yours to be expended for your good.'

This was the last occasion on which the Queen publicly addressed her subjects through Parliament, and the most notable.

Queen Elizabeth delighted in fresh air and exercise and never ate more than she needed. She must, however, have had the legendary Elizabethan sweet tooth, as this description of her shows:

'Next came the Queen, in the sixty-sixth year of her age, as we were told, very majestic; her face, oblong, fair, but wrinkled; her eyes small, yet black and pleasant; her nose a little hooked; her lips narrow, and her teeth black ... She had in her ears two pearls, with very rich drops; she wore false hair, and that red; upon her head she had a small crown ... Her bosom was uncovered, as all the English ladies have it, till they marry; and she had on a necklace, of exceeding fine jewels; her hands were small, her fingers long, and her stature neither tall nor low.'

'She took the cross-bow and killed six does and she did me the honour to give me a share of them.'

THE FRENCH AMBASSADOR AT WOODSTOCK, 1575

LEFT:
The Queen was very fond of hunting and hawking, as these illustrations from Turbeville's Manual show.

OPPOSITE PAGE:
Garden tapestry; one of the Stoke Edith needlework hangings at Montacute House depicting an Elizabethan garden of the sort that the Queen was familiar with and enjoyed.

The sovereign had her chance to lead her knights when, in May 1588, the Armada was sent by Philip II of Spain because His Most Catholic Majesty believed he was appointed by God to defend the truth against infidels and heretics, of whom the Queen of England was one. She was also the powerful ruler of a country with which Philip had tried and failed to become influential through marriage. More and more Spanish ships were being robbed by the semi-piratical actions of Drake, who had insulted Philip further by sailing through the Straits of Magellan, which the King of Spain thought of as his.

If Philip could not conquer England by marrying her Queen, he would have to do it another way, by fighting.

Unfortunately for Spain, King Philip conducted most of his business from the safety and seclusion of the monastic palace of the Escorial, issuing all his commands through letters and never meeting his commanders or letting them meet each other. He was neither a soldier nor a sailor and appointed a man completely inexperienced in the art of war as his Captain General of the High Seas – the Duke of Medina Sidonia.

Queen Elizabeth, on the other hand, suffered no such disadvantage. The captains of her ships were sailors, successful seafaring men who were quite at home in rough seas. Her speech at Tilbury displays her talents as an actress, a statesman and a queen. 'It displays the clear confidence of Elizabeth that the unity of England, which she had sought more than all else, stood at this time accomplished. With such a theme she addressed her troops, and through them the nation' (J. Hurtfield):

'My loving people, we have been persuaded
By some that are careful of our safety
To take heed how we commit ourselves to
*   armed multitudes*
For fear of treachery. Let tyrants fear.
I have always so behaved myself that,
*   under God,*
I have placed my chiefest strength and
*   safeguard*
In the loyal hearts and goodwill of my
*   subjects.*

And therefore I am come amongst you,
As you see at this time,
Not for my recreation and disport,
But being resolved, in the midst and heat
   of the battle,
To live or die amongst you all;
To lay down for my God,
And for my kingdom,
And for my people,
My honour and my blood
Even in the dust.
I know I have the body of a weak and
   feeble woman,
But I have the heart and stomach of a king,
And of a king of England too!
And think foul scorn that Parma or Spain,
Or any prince of Europe,
Should dare to invade the borders of my
   realm!'

Meanwhile, in the English Channel, the Queen's navy was assembling under Lord Howard of Effingham as Lord High Admiral. About a dozen of the English fleet were first-class race-built ships (so called because the large castles of the older galleons had been 'razed' to deck height and the result was a ship much lower to the water, easier to handle and more nimble). These led the fleet. Some of the rest were old-fashioned galleons, and some were merchantmen. The famous English captains of the Elizabethan age were in the battle – Lord Howard in the *Ark Royal*, Drake as Vice-Admiral in the *Revenge*, Hawkins as Rear Admiral in the *Victory*, Frobisher in the *Triumph*, Beeston in the *Dreadnought*, Fenner in the *Nonpareil* and Crosse in the *Hope*. Altogether there were 10,000 men and nearly 100 sail, with another 40 sail in the Thames and the Straits of Dover.

The Spanish ships were manned by soldiers because fighting in these large galleons with high castles was traditionally done at close quarters – opposing ships' crews would board one another and engage in hand-to-hand combat. This the Spaniards could not do against the new, nimble, much faster English ships. The *Golden Hind*, for example, at 21 metres was half the length of a Spanish galleass. The English fleet was commanded by sailors, not soldiers, who were extremely

LEFT:
This painting is generally thought to be contemporary with the period of the Armada invasion and may have been designed for use as a tapestry to commemorate the event.

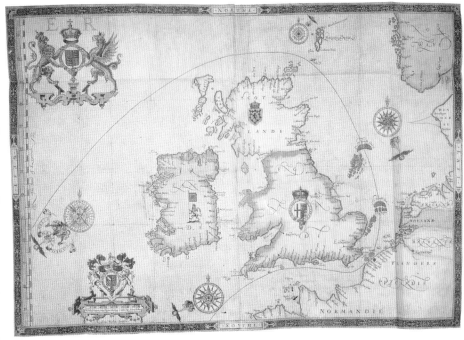

RIGHT:

After the Battle of Gravelines the Armada ran north before the wind. It was not strong enough to return through the Channel and was followed by the English up to the Firth of Forth. The Spanish ships then took the long and dangerous route home shown on this map.

BELOW:

The well-known 'Armada' portrait of the Queen at Woburn Abbey in the Elizabethan fashion pays no attention to the unities of time and space – through one window can be seen the Armada formation and through the other the storm that dissipated the Spanish fleet.

skilful in handling their trim vessels.

The Spaniards relied heavily on close-range firing of cannon to inflict damage on the hulls of galleons. This method was of no use in the Armada battles because Drake had trained his sailors to fight by handling their ships expertly. By so doing they could out-gun and out-manoeuvre the enemy.

The onshore wind in the Channel, with which the English were familiar and which enabled Drake to know whether or not he had time to finish his legendary game of bowls before setting sail to engage the enemy, was another factor very much in England's favour. 'But the final and decisive fact was that English shot, at the very shortest range, could penetrate a hull and Spanish shot could not; and the probable cause of that, unknown to the Spaniards, was that their shot was badly cast and brittle' (David Howarth, *The Voyage of the Armada*).

In the event, the Spaniards, who did not know the waters well, found themselves being chased rather than fought by the English. The guns and ammunition of the Spanish side probably did at least as much damage, in recoil, to their own ships as they did to those of the enemy. Fireships were used in the dark by the English – old ships filled with combustible material and set alight heading for the enemy: 'With eight ships they put us to flight, a thing they had not dared to attempt with a hundred and thirty.'

In the Battle of Gravelines only 30 Spanish and 40 English ships (at most) took part in the fighting, although 260 ships were present. 600 Spaniards were killed and 800 wounded, but fewer than 100 Englishmen were lost in the whole campaign. After the battle the Queen had a medal cast with the inscription:

Flavit Jehovah et dissipati sunt –
'God breathed and they were scattered.'

The cult of Elizabeth reached its zenith after the defeat of the Spanish Armada. England had defeated Spain under her great and glorious Queen – Gloriana reigned in dazzling majesty surrounded by brilliant men. William Byrd and John Dowland were composers and musicians; Sir Francis Bacon was an essayist, and Edmund Spenser a poet; Christopher Marlowe and William Shakespeare were playwrights; for a brief moment all these men were alive and working imaginatively at the same time at their several trades.

In 1576 three theatres were built in London, including the Globe, to cater for the increasingly popular theatrical entertainment. The Queen's favourite, the Earl of Leicester, had become patron of the first permanent company of players in 1574 and William Shakespeare may well have joined Lord Leicester's Men in 1587.

Music was of great importance to the Queen, who loved to dance and who was something of a musician herself. The composition of secular and church music flourished during her reign, William Byrd and Thomas Tallis being probably the Elizabethan composers most well known to us.

The art of miniature painting achieved a high degree of excellence in England in the work of Nicholas Hilliard and Isaac Oliver. There is an example of Nicholas Hilliard's work in this difficult medium on page 11.

Publishing flourished during Elizabeth's

LEFT:
Queen Elizabeth I *by Marcus Gheeraerts the Younger.*

reign as we know from the records of the Stationer's Hall, where all Elizabethan books and pamphlets had to be registered.

Elizabeth both encouraged and acted as patron to published works on historical and topographical subjects. Richard Hakluyt the Younger's *Principal Navigations, Voyages, Traffics and Discoveries of the English Nation* (1589) was an important repository of nautical intelligence. Ralph Holinshed published his Chronicles in 1577, telling the history of England from 1066 until his own day. This incorporated an introductory section describing Elizabethan England, still of great historical value today, even though it idealised Elizabeth and her reign, as did many other books of the same type.

BELOW, LEFT:
William Byrd's anthem, 'O Lord Make Thy Servant Elizabeth to rejoice in Thy Strength'.

BELOW:
A Christmas Play by Shakespeare before Queen Elizabeth *by Sir John Gilbert.*

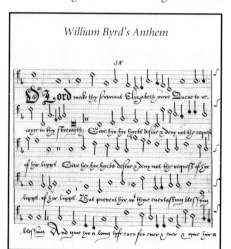

William Byrd's Anthem

Sir Francis Drake, Sir Walter Ralegh, Sir Humphrey Gilbert, Martin Frobisher, Sir John Hawkins – these great seafarers of Elizabeth's day made voyages of exploration that opened up new lands for colonisation and provided trade routes where none had existed before. Elizabeth actively encouraged these activities, well aware of the value of international trade; towards the end of her reign, in 1599, the East India Company was founded.

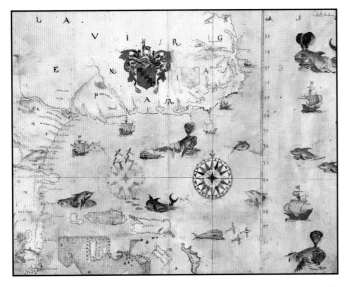

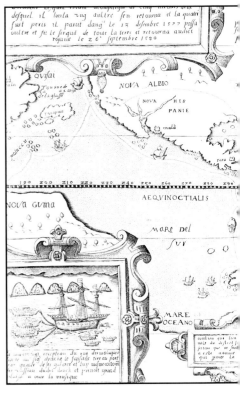

Humphrey Gilbert's *Discourse to Prove a North-West Passage*, though based on unreliable sources, instigated a wave of exploration led by Frobisher in 1576–78 accompanied by White, the artist and mapmaker. In 1581 the Levant Company was founded for trade with Turkey and a nine-year expedition led by Ralph Fitch led to trade with India and Burma.

In 1583 Gilbert set sail with a view to establishing a colony in north America. He perished in the attempt, but his half-brother, Walter Ralegh, by then a favourite with the Queen, sent out another which discovered a new land, later named Virginia in honour of Elizabeth, the Virgin Queen.

Sir Francis Drake, surely the most famous and arguably the most successful of Elizabethan mariners, circumnavigated the globe in the *Golden Hind* between 1577 and 1580. In doing this he sailed through the Straits of Magellan (because he was forced to do so by storm conditions) to the chagrin of Philip II of Spain who regarded the Straits as his. During his voyage Drake plundered Spanish

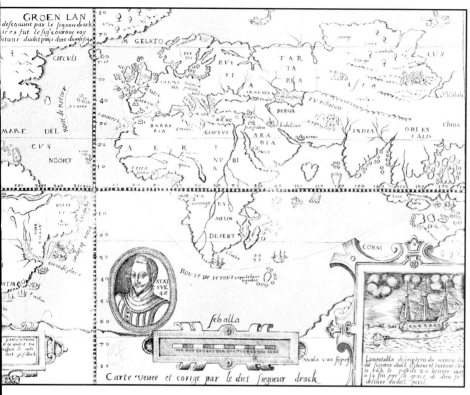

LEFT:
A map of Drake's circumnavigation of the world, engraved by Nicola van Sype, after the French original approved by Drake.

LEFT, BELOW:
An Indian of Virginia. The expedition sent out by Ralegh in 1584 returned with two Indians whom he presented to the Queen. They provided useful publicity for the colonising venture Ralegh was then preparing. The watercolour is one of many done by John White, whom Ralegh sent out with the first colonists as artist and mapmaker.

craft to the tune of £1,500,000, which represented a large portion of the entire annual yield of Philip's mines in southern America. These buccaneering acts enraged the King of Spain and contributed significantly to his decision to send the Armada to invade and conquer England.

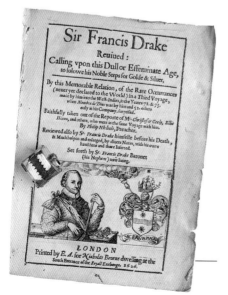

FAR LEFT:
Philip Nichol's account of Sir Francis Drake's third voyage to the West Indies. This and Drake's lodestone are at Buckland Abbey.

RIGHT:

Nonsuch Palace, near Ewell in Surrey, a favourite residence of the Queen. Nothing now remains of this most fantastic of Tudor houses. The figure in the plumed carriage in the foreground may be intended to be Elizabeth.

RIGHT:

Robert Devereux, second Earl of Essex. His stepfather, the Earl of Leicester, had been Elizabeth's favourite, and this, coupled with his good looks, must have predisposed the Queen towards him. But he was hot-headed and unwilling to play the inactive role of courtly lover to his royal mistress.

Until she was sixty and more Queen Elizabeth retained her youthful figure and her immense reserves of energy, and by careful camouflage concealed the onset of old age so that even her younger courtiers, the rising generation of Ralegh, Sidney, Essex and Mountjoy could, without too great effort, join as their fathers and uncles had joined before them, in the great love-game with the Queen. They all competed in lovers' language for her favour. She kept them dangling like so many love-sick swains. This was the way she exacted loyal service from them all and kept the factions in their place. With her 'faithful commons' in her parliaments the technique which she employed was very similar. She charmed, she flattered, she wrapped up her refusals in so much sweet-sounding verbiage that none could take offence. She never attempted to keep them at a distance, but made them welcome to her presence and gave every appearance of valuing their advice however little she was influenced by it.

Only one man was bold enough to try to pull this idol down. An idol was indeed what Elizabeth in time virtually became. The cult of the Virgin Mary was discouraged in Protestant England. The cult of the Virgin Queen bid firm to take its place. Only one man tried to shatter the illusion, and that was Robert Devereux, second Earl of Essex. Thirty-four years younger than the Queen, strong-willed and greedy for power, he often chafed under the rule of an ageing woman and lost patience with the whole silly game of courtly make-believe which obliged him to affect a lover's passion for his royal mistress. But his ultimate resort to violence in 1601 was misguided and earned him nothing but a traitor's death. He was beheaded in the Tower in 1601 because it was thought 'the Queen could never be safe as long as he lived'. Elizabeth had found it hard to sign the death-warrant of the stepson of her favourite, the Earl of Leicester, who was probably the only man for whom she had had a real affection.

The end came quite quickly for the Virgin Queen. In February 1603 the Venetian Secretary in England found her in excellent